NOW IS THE HOUR OF HER RETURN

POEMS IN PRAISE OF THE DIVINE MOTHER KALI

CLARK STRAND

ILLUSTRATIONS BY
WILL LYTLE

Monkfish Book Publishing Company
Rhinebeck, New York

Paperback ISBN 978-1-948626-74-3
eBook ISBN 978-1-948626-75-0

Library of Congress Cataloging-in-Publication Data

Names: Strand, Clark, 1957- author. | Lytle, Will, illustrator.
Title: Now is the hour of her return : poems in praise of the Divine Mother
    Kali / Clark Strand ; illustrations by Will Lytle.
Other titles: Now is the hour of her return (Compilation : 2022)
Description: Rhinebeck, New York : Monkfish Book Publishing Company, [2022]
Identifiers: LCCN 2022014379 (print) | LCCN 2022014380 (ebook) | ISBN
    9781948626743 (paperback) | ISBN 9781948626750 (ebook)
Subjects: LCSH: Kālī (Hindu deity)--Poetry. | LCGFT: Devotional poetry.
Classification: LCC PS3619.T7345 N69 2022 (print) | LCC PS3619.T7345
    (ebook) | DDC 811/.6--dc23/eng/20220407
LC record available at https://lccn.loc.gov/2022014379
LC ebook record available at https://lccn.loc.gov/2022014380

Book and cover design by Colin Rolfe

Monkfish Book Publishing Company
22 East Market Street, Suite 304
Rhinebeck, NY 12572
(845) 876-4861
monkfishpublishing.com

SAY TO THE NATIONS, *let there be no light upon the face of the Earth. Let the machines all cease their movements, the wires their humming. Let the skies be empty of satellites and silver birds. Let the forests return and the watercourses find their way. All things seek their Mother—save man only. Now is the hour of Her return.*

—THE GOSPEL ACCORDING TO THE DARK

CONTENTS

PART III

PART IV

INTRODUCTION

One morning in the early winter of 2011, I woke before dawn with a poem fully formed on my tongue. I took a notebook from the bedside table and wrote out the words without pausing to consider their content. I wanted to get them down as quickly as I could.

When I read the finished poem, I realized that I had never written anything like it before. The normal buffer between the inspiration for a poem and the poem itself was entirely absent. I wasn't sure how it had happened, and I wasn't sure I could do it again. Two days later, having failed to find the answer to this mystery within myself, I asked aloud, "How am I to do this?"

A voice replied, "To those who give hearts, words are given in return."

This was the method and the sole poetic principle I followed after that. I gave my heart to Ma Kali, and She gave me the words for these poems. If that is a bold claim, it is also a simple one. There was nothing more to it than that.

In Sanskrit, the *Ma* of Ma Kali means "Mother," while *Kali* itself means "Black." Ma Kali is therefore a "Black Mother"—a chthonic goddess as vast as the universe and, at the same time, able to chart the course of a pebble as it drifts through countless tides on its way to becoming a grain of sand.

Mother Kali is a mixture of dirt and stardust. She guides the plants and animals through vast chains of birth, death, and regeneration…and holds the orbits of the planets in Her embrace. She is the Dark Matter of the universe, and its Dark *Mater*, too—the Mother at the bottom of it all. Readers of my book *Waking Up to the Dark* will discover that she is also the Black Madonna—a figure long suppressed from the memory of modern human beings, but whose time has, at long last, finally come round again.

To understand the poems which follow, it will be helpful to know a little about that Black Mother in her Hindu incarnation—specifically, her story and the iconography associated with her statues and images.

A great cosmic battle was being fought between the gods and Raktabīja, a demon whose every drop of blood became the seed from which an identical demon would grow. There was no way to defeat this aberrant male energy by following the rules of ordinary warfare. Wounding it only made it stronger. It was the goddess Durga who finally saw the futility of this. Summoning from within herself the ultimately destructive female force, she produced Ma Kali—a dark warrior goddess who swallowed every drop of the demons' blood, annihilating them once and for all.

Sadly, once unleashed, there was no stopping that rampaging female power. To prevent the destruction of the entire universe, the god Shiva entered the field of battle and threw himself beneath Kali's feet. Finding the body of her husband beneath her, Kali returned to her senses and, with Raktabīja's army of demons now vanquished, the order of the world was restored.

In Hindu iconography, Ma Kali is usually depicted standing atop the prone body of Shiva, with one foot resting on his chest, the other upon his thigh. Her four arms brandish a sword, a spear, a human head, and a skullcup filled with blood. Her hair is wild and black (some would say matted) and so long that it trails the ground. Her neck is decked with a rosary of heads or skulls, and she wears a skirt of severed arms about her waist. Her tongue lolls from her mouth, long and bloodied, and her breasts are always gloriously, daringly bare.

And yet, it is only to the powerful, the arrogant, or the proud that Ma Kali offers such a terrifying image. To the Hindu faithful she is the gentle, sweet, and ever-loving Divine Mother, the "Queen of the Cosmos" who embraces all, forsaking none...in life and in love, as well as in destruction and death.

In closing, I will add only that Hindu mythology speaks of four *yugas* (or "world cycles") which are repeated endlessly throughout cosmological time. The last is the *Kali Yuga*, an Age of Darkness and Destruction, and the Black Mother is its mistress.

When we consider the acceleration of species extinction brought on by the Anthropocene—the "Age of Humans"—it is clear that we are now living in that time. It was only with the widespread use of fossil fuels and petro-chemicals beginning in the late nineteenth century, however, that a force like Raktabīja has appeared.

The poems which follow celebrate the Return of the Mother in both her tender and terrible aspects, for she is both of these at once and each of us gets to decide which face we see. A battle is coming, but there is no question who will win that battle in the end. The only thing to be decided is who will side with Mother in that battle...and who will stand against Her.

These Belong to You

Kali, I write these songs,
But they belong to You
To do with as You please.
I am like the bead a cord
Passes through, a field
The wind blows over,
The banks of a stream.

As long as cord and wind
And water pass through me,
That's enough. Let my words
Fall deeper each day
Into the bottomless black
Well of Mother Kali's ear.

PART I

When Bengal Came to Me

I fell asleep and woke
In Bengal. OK, that's not
Exactly how it happened
But it's what I usually
Say, because the truth is
Too shocking—which is this:

That Bengal came to me.
First She sent Her tigers
To eat me, but they did not.
Next She commanded jackals
But they, too, grew bored
And fell asleep.

Before long I had this
Whole menagerie of crazy
Creatures all sleeping
At my feet. I can't tell you
What a funk they sent up.

The cleaning lady quit,
Said, "You need Ma Kali
For this kind of work.
I can't do it.""Alright, then,"
I said. "Do you have
Her number?" And she did.

The Knowledge Roses Have

Mother, you broke through the bottom
Of the night and placed your hand in mine
And said, "This and only this awaits you."

And I was made calm as an infant who
Holds the future and the past within him,
As a seed does, but for whom the present

Is as empty as a dream. I had no thought
But breath and mountain water, no knowledge
But the knowledge roses have. And there

Were thorns there, too, I am sure of it,
That drew my blood, but I felt no pain. For
It is the blood of roses that makes them red,

And beautiful, and returns them to their
Mother—who returns them to the world.

Are You Prepared to See Me?

Mother, why is Your
Hair so long and wild?
A respectable bun might
Suit You nicely, and
Wouldn't it make the
Longings that course
Pulse-like through the
Veins in the body of
The world that much
Easier to bear?

Do you think so? asked
Kali. Easier for whom?
My true children feel no
Dread in My dreadlocks.
Besides which, are you
Prepared to see Me
Naked? Surely it hasn't
Escaped your attention
That Ma Kali wears
Nothing but Her hair.

The Night We First Made Love

The night we first made love I thought
To take Her as a man does a woman
Whose surrender is complete,
But Ma Kali said, "Not so fast!"

Next thing I knew, I was on my back.
She was crushing me with Her feet.
"Where'd You learn that?" I snapped.
"From some other lover, no doubt."

"Lord, no!" laughed Kali. "There's nothing
I don't know about dancing men to dust.
But if you keep talking you will spoil it.

If you have to talk, talk dirty. Say things
Too shameful for anyone but Kali to hear.
Do you think I blush who've suckled and

Bedded and buried you a billion times
Before now? Save your shame for some
Pious, pretty thing who likes that kind

Of love. I want a man whose heart I
Can dance on. Just be a lotus. It doesn't
Matter if your roots are in the mud."

In the Dark

I am an arrow pointed at the night—
Who knows where it goes?
This I said, but Kali only laughed:

What woman doesn't know,
Even without thinking, how to guide
Her lover in the dark?

The Weight of Every Hour

Sit down on My lap
And I'll tell you a story,
Said Kali one night.
She was speaking to Her child.

Before you were born
There were giants in the land,
And each one carried on
His back a stone the size

Of a lesser moon. Like moons
Those stones would have
Floated in place had these
Giants paused even once

To consider their plight.
The burdens they struggled
To carry through life
Were never really there.

In that way gradually, like
Mountains, they wore down
Until finally they were
The size of ordinary

Women and men. I try to tell
Them that I carry
The weight of every hour,
But they don't believe me.

What am I to do with this
Knowledge? I asked Mother.
Nothing, said She. You don't
Even have to carry that.

But I Didn't Know She Was a Woman

Kali sometimes takes me traveling
And lets me witness a thing that no one
Has ever seen before, like the time

She let me watch the Moon bathing
In the bay. "But I didn't know She was
A woman," I exclaimed. I felt betrayed.

It was as if nothing my human mother
And father had ever told me was true.
"You shouldn't blame them," said Mother.

"They're hardly responsible for not telling
You what their own mothers and fathers
Also never knew. They knew other things.

For instance, they must have told you how
The Moon orbits the Earth and the Earth orbits
The Sun. They'd simply forgotten why.

Watch how, even now, Old Sol embraces
Her body with His light. Can you not hear,
With every droplet that slides shimmering

Down Her belly, the depth of His lover's sigh?
Apart from the occasional eclipse, when they
May lie together in the shadow of the World,

It's as close as He comes to touching Her. Your
Earthly mothers and fathers have forgotten
That they, too, are lovers first and last of all.

I brought you here to remember that." She
Left me then and I looked a while longer,
Hidden as I was. If the Moon noticed me

Watching Her from the shore, She never gave
Any indication. She was too busy
Being beautiful for Her lover, clothed only in

The singular embrace of His light. Later
I wondered, is this what we have forgotten
That allows us to destroy the World?

Blue One Day and Middle Aged

I was blue one day and middle aged
And trying to decide what to spend
My life on, so it wouldn't have been a waste.

"Spend it on Me!" cried Kali Ma.
I wasn't sure what that kinds of things
That entailed and if it paid a salary or not.

"What's in it for me?" I asked.
"Or is it a worshipful, devotional
Thing where the rewards are intangible?"

"Your world is intangible," said Mother.
"Money, power, security, control.
Men waste their lives on these, and it's even

Worse when they get them.
I promise a heart to bear insult,
The courage to bear up under the wicked,

And a word to bring the powerful
To their knees. But you must bear
That word within you and never speak it.

It will be all you own, but it will
Not be yours. I agreed, and She placed
A word on my lips the weight of a galaxy.

And I swallowed it and held it
Without fear. For She told me
The powerful would not have it, and the prideful

Would perish in a day. Only I should run
And hide when She cried, "Now!"
And carry with me those whom I loved.

All That Is Lost to Me Now

Ma Kali came walking along at
Sunset. Her footsteps were like
The shadows of sticks upon
The ground. She held out Her
Hand and I took it. Woe is me
To have such a lover. For I shall
Never now depart from this
World. We are wed, She and I,
And that sweet doom that men
Call freedom that lets them
Live and die vaingloriously—
All that is lost to me now.

In its place is a pressure that
Bends the darkness as a lover
Bends her back to her lover's
Belly in the night. I couldn't be
Free of Her now if I wanted it.
You could as soon separate
The sky from its stars as
Pull us two apart. Her eyes
Have become my eyes, Her
Body my body. Though our hands
Still touch in the night.

The Night Opened Her Legs

I read somewhere the following statement:
That "One can be a faithful disciple of Jesus
Without denying the flickers of the sacred
In followers of Yahweh, Kali, or Krishna."

Flickers? Humpf! All I can say is this—
If they ever got close enough to see
Kali flicker, they'd be too damn close.
Every grass blade smolders into green

At Her approach. The bees buzz brighter
And burst in yellow flame. But She (even to cry
The word sets me slapping flown embers
From my shirt), She burns black and emits

Not one spark. All sparks because of Her.
She is their origin and destination. It's like
When the stars vanish at dawn, and some idiot
Says, "Look! The sun drove them away!"

That's just not so. What really happened
Was this: The Night opened Her legs
And with one Great Pang took them safe
Within Herself. These people! Where do they

Think they come from? Where do they think
They go? Too much thinking is what I think. I'd
Rather be struck like a match on Mother's thigh.
Just put me back in the box when I am done.

For She Is Also Seeking You

Ma Kali, I sometimes feel
That there is no one living
At the center of the world.

It's not that I'm empty
Or lacking passion, but that
Life itself drains out

The bottom of each
Moment and I don't know
Where it has gone.

Mother gathered me up
At those words, for I was
Still small then, being no

More than a child who'd
Fallen asleep over bedtime
Prayers and let his soul

Speak of the unbearable,
Pointless loneliness that
Passed for American life.

She carried me to a place
I'd never been while waking,
Although my dreaming

Child's feet knew
The floorboards right away.
There was a girl there

No more than four,
Her face as still as moonlight
On a pillow, cradled in

The crook of her arm.
"Tonight this girl's soul uttered
Prayers that answer

Your own. The soul makes
Things so simple sometimes
That even I am astounded."

But I was already swaying
On my feet, and waking
Seven states away. The last

Words Mother spoke were,
"Time is an illusion the soul
Must break through prayer.

Now pray, and seek her.
For she is also seeking you."

PART II

What Kind of Mother Does That?

Mother hasn't any clothes but
Hands and heads. I asked about these,
But She was noncommittal.

"I've lost track of who they once
Belonged to," said Kali. "All I know is
My children fly apart at the sight of Me,

And I am left to gather them up.
What else can I do
But fasten their parts about My body?

Should I abandon the dead
And love only the living?
What kind of a Mother does that?"

It's Me They Seek

I met Kali Ma one night
Coming back from Iraq.
I see You've been busy,
I said, with all those skulls
About Your neck. Most
Virgins wear garlands of
Roses. Have You ever
Thought of that?

I'm not that kind of Virgin,
Said She. Let the dying
Call their White Ones if
They want, it's Me they seek.
You won't find Fatima anywhere
Near that kind of carnage.
Her calls come to Me, We
Arranged that long ago.

These White Daughters of Mine,
They keep busy with the
Living, don't get Me wrong.
But what a mess they leave
To clean up. I can't tell you
How often I've tried to birth
A Black One into their world.
They come out White
Every time, no matter who
I lie with, or in what phase
Of the moon. There was Jesus.

And my beloved Jeanne
Of Domremy.

And, in your tradition,
That's just about it. Put these two
Together, and meditate deeply,
And see if you don't end up
Suckling at Kali's breast.

How They All Go Out

Ma Kali, You are fond of men
At the end of life who have
Lost their superior attitude.
You don't even say, "I told you so!"

I've watched them start, then struggle,
Then grow weightless in Your embrace,
The breath atomic, the body a sunny hilltop
From which the breezes arrive and depart.

It has taken much watching, but now
I know the secret of Your arms:

The first hand stills the palsy. The second
Smooths the hair. The third flips the pages
Of a book no longer read. The last offers
The milk of Kali's breast.

It's how they all go out, whoever they've been
In life, and whatever it is they've done. In the end
They remember what they forgot in the middle:
That going out is the same as coming in.

A Dropped Stone

I am the pebble plopped into a well,
Let me fall forever if it pleases Kali Ma.
What can a pebble do but seek its Mother,
Whether falling or lying on the ground?
I sang this song, but Kali made it simpler:

Don't you remember where I found you?
Since then I've carried you all about
In My little satchel of bits and bones.
Isn't it enough when I and My Daughters
Delight in handling you at play?

That Night You Lost Your Cloak

These days I sit distracted,
Stand with my hand
On the doorknob
With nowhere to go.
I keep thinking there's
Something I've forgotten,
But who can say
What it is?

I asked Kali Ma for help, but
She also drew a blank.
Then finally yesterday
She said, "Do you remember
That night you lost your cloak
And we lay naked
Under only
A blanket of stars?

And then you rose
And said, 'I'll do this thing,
And never be parted
From You again!' Well,
That was months ago
And I can't recall the exact
Hillside, but don't
They burn bodies there?"

When I'm Gone

Kali Ma, when I am lonely You draw me
Like a child or a lover to the hollow of
Your breasts. I don't have to decide which.
You've never asked me to state my intentions.

When I'm gone they'll say this: He wasn't
Much to look at, but good God did he love
That woman! What he saw in a girl festooned
With skulls and severed arms is anyone's guess.

Two Can Play That Game

Ma Kali brought a dream in a box
And set it down between us.
"Don't you want to open it?" said She.

"As long as it's closed,
I can go on dreaming," said I,
"And You'll remain here by my side."

"You'll have to open it sometime,"
Said Mother. "Life is dreaming
And waking, only to wake and dream

Again. You couldn't stop it
If you tried. Even death can't
Stop it." I thought about this for awhile

And finally I did open it, waking
In my bed. Kali was gone,
And the box was empty, too.

That night I lingered at the edge
Of wakefulness, like a child
Unwilling to fall asleep, on my lips the words,

"Mother, two can play that game."

The Festival of Bones

Ma Kali carried me to Africa to witness
The Festival of Bones. I'd never heard
Of it before: it wasn't in any guidebook
I had read. "You won't find this day

Celebrated in the World of Men,"
Said Mother. "This happened long ago.
Or long ahead. It scarcely matters
Which. Your body can't go that far

Without flying apart like a potsherd
And lying forever where it falls. But
The more you visit the place in dreams
The less fearful you will find it being

Pulled together into a body, then
Pulled apart and moved through other
Bodies and back again to the beginning.
This is Time So Big even the gods just

Leave well enough alone. Shiva said
It was just like tilling a mountain with
A plough the size of a flea. It takes
A really long time so what's the use

Of fretting?" Still, I wondered who these
People were, and whose bones they
Celebrated. I thought about it for a while
And decided…it was better not to ask.

Where Else Could I Go?

Ma Kali, having You
Is like having a tiger
For a Mother. I don't
Mean the kind who
Pushes her child to
Become president,

Or an egomaniac, or
Both. There are tigers
And there are Tigers.
Your tongue could lick
The varnish off the world
With a single swipe.

It's not comfortable
Lying next to You
At night, but honestly
Where else could I go?
Who would lie elsewhere
When they've lain

With Kali Ma? Best not
Ask such questions
Anyway. There's no road
Back to the world
From Mother...when no one
Wants to come back.

Brother Louis

I wouldn't want the fate
That befell Merton to fall
To me, so I am writing
This tonight. I'm not talking
About electrocution.
Who cares about that?
Not me. Not Merton even. Not
Even then. The thought that must
Have passed in a flicker as
Every circuit burned bright
Was this: They will use me for
The Father, and cut the Mother
Out. Damn! Who expects to be
Electrocuted on
The way to meet his lover? Hard luck,
But a lesson to me. Thanks,
Brother Louis, Father Tom!
I'll watch your back the next
Time we all come around.

The Ride of the Cosmos

My Mother, Daughter
Sister, Lover, Bride is One
With all qualities. It's
Pointless trying to find
A thing
That She is not.

I pour myself out
Each day, turn
Inward each night, turn
Flips and somersaults
At Her feet
Like Shiva.

I am barely conscious
During this. I'm along
For the ride of the Cosmos.
She stands with one
Foot planted firmly
On my chest,

The other holds my
Thigh, the weight of Her
Like so many
Stars pulled inside out,
Made fine and perfect
In their fall.

I become mass only, so
Light I become dark, so
Dark I become light again.
The broken heart
Of a galaxy
Is a universe complete.

So let me put these
Questions before you: They
Must be answered. Who
Can survive Her? Who
Can be without Her?
Tell me if you can.

In the Sun

I found Ma Kali
Meditating in a field
In the sun. It was

An anomaly.
She rarely ever let me
See Her in the light.

I went a long time
Thinking She was a creature
Of the night, but then

One morning I woke
With Her smiling at my side.
Still, She wouldn't speak

Unless it was dark.
The night is for listening,
She whispered once, and

For other acts that don't
Belong to daylight, like Love
And Revelation.

But meditation…
That can be done in the sun,
Where no one expects

To be spoken to
By God or a Beloved
Or touched in naked

Places like the Soul.
Haven't you ever noticed
Daylight makes Me clothed?

PART III

Show Me the Man Who Will Listen

Ma Kali, what servants You must have
That you can lavish so many on my education!
That You've sent seven women can't speak well
Of me. Surely one or two should have been

Enough to set an ordinary sinner to rights.
Don't You have anyone else whose heart needs
Reconnoitering? "The number of women,"
Said Mother, "who want this work is greater

Than you imagine. They say, 'Show me the man
Who will listen and I will depart for his world
At once—he need not even listen well or long!'"
"It's the miracle of low expectations," said Kali.

That put things in perspective, though it didn't
Change me one iota. I wore my thoughtful
Listening look for seven days after that. Then
Mother said, "Enough! Be what you are.

But know that most would give their lives
For you, and some of them already have.
When you have seen the misery of women
For what it is, the world shall be remade. Men

Think the work of creation is shaping a stone
Into a tool, and then a tool into a world. Try
Shaping that stone inside your belly and then
Birth it, and watch it shatter on the ground."

Her Patience Is at an End

I snuck Kali Ma into a church
To show Her the Blessed Virgin
And said, "Mother, what do You
Think of that?"

"She's beautiful," said Kali,
"But Her patience is at
An end. Don't suppose
She can't become

Black at a moment's notice.
You see only Her piously
Prayerful hands. Of the other
Two, one plots

The fall of Wall Street,
The other takes the pulse
Of the pope, counting down his
Seconds like

A bomb. Because his death
Is a sign of the end."

Who Is Her Father?

Some scholars came and asked,
"What right have you to take
Ma Kali as your bride?
You never asked Her hand, never
Visited Her Father's home."

So I asked them, "Who is Her Father,
Whom you profess to know so well?
Answer me that and I will openly
Renounce Her,
And you may have Her back at once."

But that struck them speechless,
Just as Ma Kali said it would.
She snickered and made faces
For hours after that
And kept sticking out Her tongue

If Only It Were That Easy

Ma Kali, the man I sent
To visit You was shocked
To find You naked when he arrived.

I tried to remember
How I felt that first time.
I wasn't shocked exactly, but it did

Make me wonder
What Your expectations
Were. Now, of course, I know.

There's no point in
Pretending as a man
That Ma Kali isn't what we want.

And yet, how long
It took to get naked,
And honest, and willing to let

You do to me
What was necessary
To save my living soul. Truth is,

I think he thought
You wanted to bed him.
If only it were that easy,

I wanted to say.

An Eight-Year-Old Girl

Once I arrived to meet Mother
Only to find that She had left
An eight-year-old girl minding
The shop. This isn't some job

You can take time off from,
I thought to myself. There are rivers
To bend and seasons to turn
Upon the vast, elastic lathe

Of the world. But all things Ma Kali
Did, this girl did just as well. It was
Astounding to watch. Her small
Hands moved like Mother's.

I returned the following night,
And there was Kali as before,
Busy with the deft and discerning
Business of the world. "Do You

Often skip out like that?" I asked.
"And who was that You left in
Your place?" But Mother said not
One word in reply. I looked more

Deeply then, and eventually saw
Her again, that girl. She was always
There, as close and dark as a shadow
At Mother's side. She never spoke.

She didn't need to. Her role was
To learn everything from Mother,
And never to question or doubt.
She was trust incarnate. It was how

She learned everything so easily,
And remembered all she was told.
I was in awe of her, knowing I could
Never be like that. But Mother read

My mind: "You've no business
Comparing yourself to this child,
Who is My apprentice, but you might
Have told her a story or invited

Her to play. The father you could be
Would have recognized at once
What a lonely role she plays. It's true
I left her in charge of the world.

But I left you in charge of her."

I Do Not Forget

Mother Kali, is it all right
To say a rosary to You?
The priests say
You are at war
With the church.

I am at war
With priests, says Mother.
My White Daughters are bound
So fast They forget, but I…
I do not forget.

Now I will wake Them
And I shall take Them
And bake Them black
And make Them mighty
And slake Their thirsting.

When the milk
Of the night lets down,
The stars will fall
To lie with men
Once more and be their lovers.

Now Is the Hour of Her Return

Kali Ma arrived last night from Canada
Without Her sword. It was the only place
She could get in. The borders had been closed.

"Mother, you're defenseless now," I cried.
"The people here won't respect a naked
Village girl with empty hands and pockets

And hair so long it trails the ground—
We must hide You on an altar somewhere."
But Kali said, "That's not what I intend.

For when they seize My hand to take Me
And bind Me to their oblivion, that's just
When I begin to dance. You're too young

To remember a time that happened
At the close of an age, when men forgot
Their Maker. I always come like this,

My defenseless body an invitation
They will never be able to resist.
I am the knife too sharp for any sheath.

Do they suppose I have forgotten
How their bones were put together?
Every good cook maid knows her meat."

Call Me Mother

I heard a voice that said,
You have tainted Kali Ma!
For days I was so ashamed
I could barely call Her name.

Finally, She found me hiding
And said, I hold you close
And sing and whisper things
I never tell even the righteous.
Don't you think I deserve a call?

What is true of an ordinary girl
Is also true of Kali Ma.
Would you hold Me distant?
Would you have Me indifferent?

An infant cries and the milk
Lets down. The same is true
For Kali and Her lovers.
If you love Me, call Me Mother,
Daughter, Sister, Lover, Bride.
Treat Me like a Beloved
If you want to feel My embrace.

The River of the Dead

In an early morning vision, Mother
Carried me to the river that marks
The boundary between the worlds.

There I saw three women who faced
Away from me—respectfully, I thought—
For their backs were naked, and to gaze

Upon them when they turned carried
Certain inevitable obligations.
I would know things that could not

Be known, for these were not ordinary
Naked women a man might stumble upon
And remark later, "I saw these beauties,

Just there by the water!" To see them
Was to submit to something irrevocable.
But then one of them spoke and said,

"Only ask and we shall turn, and you may
Look upon us, but we would not force such
Knowledge upon the living." To Kali I said,

"Mother, what am I to do? I haven't even
The sense to know what is being offered me."
Said Kali Ma: "They have offered the truth

In a false world. Would you presume
To come by that knowledge another way?"
It was enough. I gave my consent.

They turned, pale and silent and beautiful,
And led me with soft words and caresses
That pulled the flesh from my bones like

Well-cooked meat, and I left it there beside
The waters to come back for later, when I passed
Once more over the River of the Dead.

The Long Black Body of the Dark

It is deep night and Mother is
Using all four hands and twenty
Fingers to scratch matches against
The long black body of the dark.

The meteors are relentless, come
One after another in such quick
Succession there is no time to
Make sense of them. No sooner

Have I cried, "Ah! Would you look
At that!" than another wonder
Flashes in a heartbeat through
The sky. This is a vision, of course.

There are no Perseids or Leonids
Tonight. Mother has simply turned
My eyeballs inside out and inscribed
Herself a tattoo across my soul.

These lights will go on, needle
Bright, until dawn and then Ma Kali
Will lay me to rest within myself
Until She has need of me again.

Mother, how can You give so much
Beauty to one man without killing
Him? Or is that Your intention?
I realize now I've never asked.

The Time of the End

Mother, I have folded my words flat
As You told me and sealed them fast
So they cannot be opened until
The time of the end. But I want to ask

You what's the point of this, because
I can't see what purpose there is in making
A prophecy that doesn't prophesy
Anything, but simply points at a stone

Lying where it has fallen on the ground
And says, "There! That is the very place
It was always destined. These things have
Been determined!" People will look at me

With scorn and say I wasn't a prophet
After all. "You never spoke to Kali Ma,"
They'll say. "Now leave us to the misery
Of all that we remember of the world!"

But Mother told me I hadn't understood
Her true intent. "These words are for you
Alone. You are to open them and read them
On that day, and know that all things I have

Told you would come to pass have occurred
As I said they would. And therefore you will
Believe what I tell you now, that you will be
The first of a people who will believe

What Mother says and no longer fear Her
Or cover Her body or close Her mouth. But
You will love Her and listen to all that She
May say, and never flee from Her embrace."

Said the Moon, Remembering

I found the Moon out wandering one night
The way the Moon will when She is full
And restless and has nothing to do but wait
For the month to diminish Her. "Little girl,
Are you lost?" I asked. (I was being playful.)

"No," she answered. "I'm just looking at
The world and wondering at how few people
Look up anymore. It's as if I don't exist.
As if they could get by without looking at
The Moon. I could tell them the things that

Only the Moon can. Like how many days
They have left of life, or how to know
The meaning of their dreams. Does Mother
No longer instruct them, I wonder?"
"No, it's not that," I answered, "Ma Kali talks

Only of You. But men no longer listen. It's
Because their time is near. From now until
The end they will attend only to themselves.
But Mother has foretold all this. How can it be
You did not know?"

              Said the Moon,
Remembering, "I guess I knew,
But it was so long ago, and I kept hoping
That somewhere someone would look up.
Isn't that what you hope for, too?"

But I was a man like all the others,
Except that I happened to remember Ma Kali
Myself that night and the things She had
Spoken to me in dreams—and so I was
Able to talk to the Moon as men once did.

At dawn I would go back to being myself
And forget all this. Except that I wrote a poem.

PART IV

The Glances that Pass Between You

Who should I show these poems
To, Kali Ma? I have a friend
Who reads them. And there's my wife.
She knows You, too. I'd show
Them to my daughter, but then
Her hair would grow wild, her
Teeth too white and sharp. My son
Would try to wed You. Who can resist You?

In the end, I've had to make
My own decision. For now there'll be
These two—wife and friend. He needs
Them, reads them like the formula
For a medical compound
That would kill an unafflicted mind.

And my beloved, of course. She's why
You came to begin with. You haven't
Said so much, either of you, but I'm
Not as stupid as I look. I see the glances
Pass between you. It was she
Who brought You. I never sought You.

Appear to him thus, she said,
And he will seize and master You,
And, please, Kali Ma, for my sake
You must let him, for he is
Stubborn and, after all, a man
And will not know
That he has been colluded upon.

Once You have him, I must
Trust to Your discretion.
You may take him to save him—
I know the things You must do.
After that, Mother-Sister, I'd like
To have him back for a while.

Find a Girl and Love Her

Ma Kali woke me and said,
Get drunk tonight and dance
With everyone you meet,
And by morning you will have
A life well worth the dying.

You keep asking for the secret.
Well, here it is. Hold nothing
In reserve. Empty your pockets
And your heart. Find a girl
And love her. But whatever

You do, don't complain. Wine
Won't defile you. Dancing is good
For the heart. And women are
Holy, even the bad ones, but
Loneliness is a sin against the gods.

Such A One

Kali Ma, You woke me,
Said, "Get up! Get going!
There's love to make,
For you must take
Me by the Neck, the Hair,
The Heart of Me.
Whatever Part of Me
You wish is yours."

What man wouldn't rise
To such an invitation?
You know us well enough.
For fifteen years
You left me sleepless,
And for all the prayers
In the universe
Never once appeared.
What were you thinking?
It nearly destroyed us both.

Well…me, anyway.
When at last I saw You,
You were young
And ageless
And august
And empty of all
But want and wonder.

And you were right
To make me wait
So long, and slay me
So many times over—
And so very, very slow.

What man can know
Before his body is broken
How his soul
Should love such a One?

Here's What Really Happened

My body was a bow,
My soul an arrow
Pointed at the dark.

Anyway, that's how
I once described it.
But that was wrong.

Here's what really
Happened: That night,
When my erstwhile

Arrow should have flown
At the dark, it dropped
And clattered at Kali's feet.

She was never far.
The distance I imagined
Was never really there.

I'm Smaller Than That Now

Kali Ma is slight, but I am smaller:
I can dart between Her legs and hide
Behind Her skirt. Her arms are always
Plucking me out of trouble
And setting me down where I belong.
Life was always hard when I was larger.
I'm smaller than that now.

Call Me On Your Own Bones

Ma Kali told me She lacked for nothing
But it would please Her if I called "Jai Kali!"
On the white bone beads of my rosary.

"Or call Me on your own bones," She added,
"Which are even better than that."

Kali's Box

Ma Kali opened Her box, and out
Popped Jesus. I know that seems
An outrageous claim, but those men
Wouldn't have listened to a woman
If the Queen of Heaven Herself
Had told them what was what.

Well, I guess they didn't listen
To Jesus either. But at least they
Learned they couldn't kill Him and make
Him stay dead. Kali's box is a coffin
With two lids. There's absolutely
Nothing you can bury that stays put.

Hide-and-Seek

I asked Ma Kali about
Her favorite game:
Did She have one,
What was it, and
How did you play?

"I like hide-and-seek
Best of all," She said.
"You hide, I seek you,
And when I find you,
The game begins again."

Said I, "A wise rabbi
Taught that God hides
So men will seek Him.
Your game is just
The opposite of that."

Said Kali, "The Father
Is always disappearing
For a season or a night.
Not so Kali. Men
Disappear, but not

The Mother. Meditate
On this truth, and
Run fast or slow
As you like. Kali
Will find you in the end."

You Did This to Yourself?

I met Ma Kali out walking in the night.
Her whole body was tattooed with stars:
Even Her eyelids and the bottoms of Her feet.

Wherever the dark was, stars were,
And wherever the stars were, like a lover
The dark was, too. There were tattoos

Within tattoos, and tattoos within those
Tattoos, too. They went on forever, and
They were forever. I was astounded.

"You did this to Yourself?" I asked.
"It must have hurt!" But Mother only laughed.
"It hurts the first time with the Father,

But what of that? Each bit of black
In the heavens is a Mother and a Lover, and I
Am all of these, and Myself as well.

But it's a brief and perfect pain, pulling them
Through My body to the other side of light."
She waived Her arm then and something like

A ripple carried my soul so far from itself
It didn't know know from knowing.
And I stopped and wasn't anymore.

But then it brought me back.

For Lo, I Have Quieted Myself

How can I flee You, Mother?
Does a stone flee the river?
The grass blade the field
That bore it? I could stray

And make You chase me,
I suppose, but what would be
The point? "For lo! I have
Quieted myself like a child

On his Mother's breast," said
The Psalmist. "Like a weaned
Child is my soul within me."
Of course, he spoke of You

And not some metaphor
For God. For men never turn
Breasts into a metaphor,
Which is a sin, even for poets.

In every scripture that still
Makes sense of the world,
You stand at the center
And You are the center,

And everything else besides.

Take the Mississippi, For Example

Once I was wondering how it would be
To be born in another body, in another
Place and time. I'd have had a different
Mother, and different brothers, and

Different sisters, too. The sky would be
The same when I looked up, but nothing
Else. Life would have been reshuffled
By some Cosmic Tarot-Telling Riverboat

Gambler with different cards on top. It
Was a reverie that lasted for forty years.
Then I looked at this life, and it seemed
New for the time I'd spent away from it.

Had I been away from it? I couldn't tell.
It was like everything and everyone in it
Had been picked up and moved, and then
Set down again in a different state.

It's a hard thing to explain, how accepting
Life essentially reinvents it. I asked Mother
How this was possible, and She said I'd
Only discovered a secret Her creatures

Already understood. The world and everything
In it passed through seasons of remembering
And forgetting and remembering what
It knew. "Take the Mississippi, for example.

That great Mother Serpent moves wriggling
Everywhere at once upon the vast, dark
Belly of a nation, forgetting Herself for long,
Long stretches, and then remembering again.

When that happens, She floods so deep and
Wide that the life of every creature for miles
Is only about that. Then they just pick up
Sticks and float, eventually arriving at

All-new destinations, only to discover that
They are really one in the same. The place
They left and the place they've arrived are
All One Mother. It's because the River,

That Great Mississippi, has swept up all
The soil and water and everything else Her
Children need, just like a woman shelling
Snapbeans in her apron for the pot.

Wherever they settle, those birds and insects,
And animals of every kind—well, they've
Got what they need for a Life…dreams,
And wisdom, and the milk that men call dirt

And brush from their boots like a thing
They ought to get rid of or get off of them.
Where do they want to get to? I ask
Myself. And who will carry them if not Me?

They call Nature a Mother (and therefore
A woman) not because they know it to be
A Truth So Old you could trace it back to
The beginning, but because they want to

Dismiss Her and get back to their business.
But that never works for long. A River that
Mighty will forget Herself for good stretches
Because She can. Her Work requires no

Thought or deliberation, but only Love.
And that She can perform in the drowsiest
Of dream-states, like when a woman
Lets down her milk and her defenses, becoming

A river in and of herself. But eventually
Feeding time is done, and the waters rise,
And the Children of Men run madly through
The streets of all those shady, erstwhile

Peaceful Delta towns crying, 'The Day
Of the LORD is at hand.' It's all fuss
And nonsense. It's just a Mother waking
And remembering Her children,

And moving them all about."

To Lay One's Heart Upon the Ground

Mother, tonight I have taken my heart
From its cage and laid it at Your feet.
The rapture of this was indescribable.

For one thing, I didn't die as I thought.
I discovered that hearts were for giving
And not for having. This was the first

Lesson of the night. The second came
When I understood what it felt like
To lay one's heart upon the ground.

I wept to think how many years of life
I wasted not knowing where a heart
Belonged. Those were lessons enough,

But then You rested Your foot upon me
And I saw the Universe from the bottom up
The only way it could be witnessed.

That was as much as I could bear,
And there was no lesson in it, for it was
More than anyone could learn.

In the end I've decided to leave
This heart in Your keeping. Do with it just
What You do with the Universe,

And that will be good enough for me.

AFTERWORD

Several years have passed since I wrote the poems for *Now Is the Hour of Her Return*. The book was originally to have been published in 2014, but somehow the final pieces of the project—from the design, to the art, to the precise ordering of the poems—never quite came together. Other books were published in the interim. And still others were contracted with publishers and begun.

Eventually, I had to admit that, small as it was, I was reluctant to send this particular book out into the world. The time was not yet right. The "now" of *Now Is the Hour of Her Return* hadn't yet arrived.

Here are the facts behind the book, its origin and its purpose as a collection of poems. Since a longer version of the story can be found in *Waking Up to the Dark*, and a still longer one in *The Way of the Rose: The Radical Path of the Divine Feminine Hidden in the Rosary*, co-authored with my wife Perdita Finn, I will be brief.

In the early hours of June 16, 2011, I witnessed an apparition of the Divine Feminine in Her form as the Virgin Mary. She appeared as a young girl with an X of black electrical tape covering Her mouth. I removed the tape, after which we continued to gaze at one another for a long time. Then She was gone.

When She appeared again two weeks later, I had prepared a question for Her. "Who are you?" I asked.

"I am the Hour of God," She replied—an appellation with apocalyptic overtones that escaped me at the time.

From the night of the first apparition, She never left my side. I witnessed Her visual form rarely, but I felt Her presence and Her touch constantly. And She would speak to me at odd moments—in the beginning usually only at night.

Eventually, I began keeping a small notebook in my pocket in which to write down the things She said.

> *"Did you think there would be no hand to take yours when you reached into the dark? Did you think you were an only? Did you feel alone?"*

> *"The rosary is My body, and My body is the body of the world. Your body is one with that body. What cause could there be for fear?"*

> *"You will not find what you seek—but Who."*

I realized that She had been speaking like this all my life and I'd simply refused to listen. Much later She would say: "About that first night when you removed the tape from My mouth: You must realize by now that I would never allow anyone to cover My mouth. The tape you removed was in your heart."

For the first few years I understood very little of this. At first, I didn't even know who She was. One night toward the end of that first summer She woke me with the words, "If you rise to say the rosary tonight, a column of saints will support your prayer." Her mention of the rosary confirmed what I had already begun to suspect. I wasn't Catholic, or even Christian, but I also wasn't stupid—there was only one figure who invited you to pray the rosary and made promises based on whether you accepted that invitation or not.

The problem was, She didn't seem anything like the Blessed Virgin Mary of the Church. For one thing, She was too powerful to fit inside of the traditional Marian mold. For another, She never spoke of sin or Jesus or the importance of going to Mass. If anything, She seemed disinterested, even slightly bored, when it came to matters concerning the Catholic Church.

Perhaps most shocking, there was nothing particularly virginal about Her. Quite the opposite. She manifested the energy and power of sex itself, albeit on a cosmic scale. This aspect of Her presence was overwhelming at times, as I think these poems make clear. Writing them was the only release from that tension I could find. Because, of course, whatever Greek myth might say to the contrary, you can't make love to the Goddess as a mortal and expect to live to tell the tale.

The erotic language of the poems in *Now Is the Hour of Her Return* is therefore metaphorical. To express the feeling of being so fully overwhelmed by the presence of One who is so fully Other, love was the only language that would suffice. I am not alone in the use of such language. The Lover of the Song of Songs used it to describe his Beloved, as did Bernard of Clairvaux in his writings about Mary and the Bengali mystics Ramprasad and Sri Ramakrishna in their hymns to Kali Ma.

It was finally there, in the Kali tradition, that I found the language to describe those first encounters with the Divine Mother. Part diary, part spiritual self-exploration, the poems of *Now Is the Hour of Her Return* record a broad range of experiences. But they do so spontaneously. The poems were never labored over. Even the longest were completed in little more than the time it would take to write them down. Often, I was taking dictation from the Mother Herself.

Two weeks before the 2016 election, Perdita and I hosted Will Lytle for dinner to discuss the illustrations for the book. Afterwards, as we were preparing for bed, Perdita said, "Well, I guess we're finally ready to go to press." But Mother said, "Not quite. I have a difficult decision to make that has a bearing on the timing for the release of this book."

A little nervous at the sound of that, we asked what that decision entailed, and She replied, "I have to decide whether to come down on My right foot or My left."

This should have made sense to us at the time, but it didn't. The poems had long since accomplished what our Mother intended them to do. By the time I finished writing them, Ma Kali had so greatly deepened and expanded our understanding of the Virgin Mary, we no longer needed to refer to the Indian spiritual tradition to make sense of Her.

The Virgin Mary stood in a direct line of descent from those Paleolithic mother goddesses from twenty thousand to thirty thousand years ago excavated by archaeologists across Central Europe. These were the "Great Grandmothers" not only of Inanna, Isis, and Aphrodite, but of Parvati, Durga, and Ma Kali as well. Kali remained on the mantel next to our medieval statue of the Virgin Mary once we understood this, and from time to time we uttered Her mantra, but it was the latter we made our prayers to from one day to the next.

The night She told us about Her pending "decision," She sent us back to the Kali tradition for a brief refresher course in Hindu iconography. There we discovered a detail we hadn't noticed in our earlier reading. If Kali stands with Her right foot resting upon Shiva's chest, that posture indicates Her manifestation as Loving Mother. If, however, She rests Her left foot upon Her husband, she becomes the embodiment of Vengeful Wrath. Right foot means Mother, left foot means Destroyer. I will leave the reader to interpret the course of events since November 2016 and what they mean in terms of the Divine Mother's intentions where human beings are concerned.

In closing, I will add something the Divine Mother said on October 28 of that year, when Election Day was still two weeks away. This is my way of giving Her the last word on this book and the prophetic dimension of its poems. They were always Hers to do with as She pleased:

> *It is important to remember that the order you fear losing is really disorder. You must always pray for the Earth to win. This one prayer is the answer to all others. When people are able to understand this, all their dreams will come true.*
>
> *Until then, the most they can hope for is to trade dreams with one another as a kind of currency. This is what you call culture, and cultures tend to revolve around money. But money has nothing whatsoever to do with the Earth.*
>
> *Thus, it is wise not to fear the loss of order. Order must be lost. That is because the human ordering of the world is really dis-order. Naturally, this will be difficult for you to accept.*
>
> *My right foot is My left foot, and My left foot is My right. My kind, motherly demeanor towards human beings might be taken as left-footed by the natural world. Whereas My wrathful, destructive nature toward humans, from the point of view of plants and other animals, might be seen as a return to the natural order. Thus, what seems good to you may actually be bad, what seems bad may really be good.*
>
> *I am a Mother who carries the world through time, stepping now on one foot, now on another. But you must know that on that journey I also carry you. Nothing, and no one, will ever be left behind.*

HAIL MARY!

JAI KALI MA!

ABOUT THE AUTHOR

A former senior editor at *Tricycle: The Buddhist Review*, **Clark Strand** is the author of books on spirituality and religion, including *Seeds from a Birch Tree*, *Meditation Without Gurus*, *How to Believe in God*, *Waking the Buddha*, and *Waking Up to the Dark*. His writing has appeared in the *Wall Street Journal*, the *New York Times*, and the *Washington Post*. Together with his wife, Perdita Finn, Strand is the author of *The Way of the Rose: The Radical Path of the Divine Feminine Hidden in the Rosary* and the co-founder of a non-sectarian rosary fellowship with members around the world.

ABOUT THE ILLUSTRATOR

The illustrator of *Waking Up to the Dark* and *The Way of the Rose*, **Will Lytle** grew up in the Catskill Mountains, where, after years as a hitchhiking, train-hopping vagabond, he returned to build a small house with wood from his family's lumber mill. Lytle is an accomplished illustrator and mural artist and the creator of the guerilla-style Thorneater Comics series.